HEART-HEALTHY

sweets & desserts

dr jehanne ali

mc Marshall Cavendish
Cuisine

Designer: Adithi Khandadai
Series Designer: Bernard Go Kwang Meng

Published by Marshall Cavendish Cuisine
An imprint of Marshall Cavendish International

Other Marshall Cavendish Offices:
Marshall Cavendish Corporation. 99 White Plains Road, Tarrytown NY 10591-9001, USA • Marshall Cavendish International (Thailand) Co Ltd. 253 Asoke, 12th Flr, Sukhumvit 21 Road, Klongtoey Nua, Wattana, Bangkok 10110, Thailand • Marshall Cavendish (Malaysia) Sdn Bhd, Times Subang, Lot 46, Subang Hi-Tech Industrial Park, Batu Tiga, 40000 Shah Alam, Selangor Darul Ehsan, Malaysia

Marshall Cavendish is a trademark of Times Publishing Limited

National Library Board, Singapore Cataloguing-in-Publication Data
Ali, Jehanne.
Heart-healthy sweets & desserts / Dr Jehanne Ali. – Singapore : Marshall Cavendish Cuisine, [2013]
pages cm
ISBN : 978-981-4398-55-8 (paperback)

1. Heart – Diseases – Diet therapy – Recipes. 2. Desserts. 3. Confectionery. 4. Cookbooks. I. Title. II. Series: Mini cookbooks.

TX714
641.56311 -- dc23

OCN829056899

Printed in Singapore by Saik Wah Print Media Pte Ltd

contents

HEART-HEALTHY
sweets & desserts

introduction

With cardiovascular diseases afflicting a growing number of people, it is essential that we scrutinise our lifestyle and do our best to maintain good health. Together with regular exercise and proper lifestyle management, a heart-healthy diet is pertinent to ensure that risk factors for heart diseases are eliminated. Specific conditions such as high blood pressure, adult onset diabetes and high cholesterol levels contribute directly to damaging blood vessels in the heart, which may lead to a heart attack and even sudden death. Diet, if managed poorly, can become a risk factor for heart diseases. What we need is a heart-healthy diet. We need foods that not only prevent the occurrence of high blood pressure, diabetes or high cholesterol levels, but superfoods that promote the well-being of the heart and possibly, repair the damage that was already done.

- *Consume foods that are rich in antioxidants regularly.*
  Berries such as strawberries, raspberries and blueberries are rich in natural antioxidants. Antioxidants prevent natural damage to the blood vessels and hence, in the long run, also help prevent formation of plaque in our coronaries. Tea, especially green tea, is a powerful antioxidant that has been scientifically proven to be able to promote longevity and improve overall well-being.
- *Incorporate the right amount of good fat in your diet.*
  Many have a misconception that fats are bad for health. While bad fats should be avoided, good fats like extra virgin olive oil, rapeseed or canola oil are now proven to be beneficial for the heart, and those are the oils that should be incorporated into our diet.
- *Eat the right kind of chocolate.*
  Moderation is key, and it is important to choose the right kind of chocolates to eat. Dark Chocolate is rich in antioxidants that prevent free radical formation, which damages heart vessels. The French Paradox diet theory recommends eating one small piece of chocolate with at least 56% cocoa a day to dramatically reduce the risk of heart diseases. A little tip: Eating citrus fruits with chocolate helps to increase the absorption of vitamins within the body.
- *Eat lots of fruits and vegetables.*
  Generally, all fruits and vegetables are good for you, but some are better than others. Pomegranate contains punicalagin, which is rich in antioxidants. Broccoli prevents free radical scavengers from damaging the coronaries. Tomatoes are chock-full of lycopene, which is good for the heart.

- *Eat more oily fish, and eat less red meat.*
  Oily fish such as salmon, tuna or mackerels are full of omega-3 fatty acids, and should be included at least three times a week in your diet.
- *Use herbs and spices to substitute salt and artificial flavourings.*
  Herbs such as parsley, thyme and oregano are so versatile and full of flavours, they not only enhance meals but also reduce the need for a higher amount of salt in the dish. Stay away from preservatives and flavourings such as monosodium glutamate. Spices such as turmeric, cayenne pepper, coriander and fennel are known to promote good health and prevent cancer. In fact, studies have shown that 2 Tbsp cayenne pepper can stop an ongoing heart attack, acting even faster than the recommended dose of aspirin!
- *Include legumes, beans and nuts in your diet.*
  There are just too many to choose from. To name a few, lentils, kidney beans, quinoa and chickpeas all contain fibres and minerals. The good news is, they are low in fat too.
- *Eat eggs in moderation.*
  Some health institutions advise that having one egg a day is good for maintaining overall well-being. It is alright to consume egg whites, but try to limit consumption of egg yolks to just two a day.

If you choose the right foods, you keep your body fit and your heart healthy. You can enjoy three delicious meals and even desserts too!

For more heart-healthy recipes, check out other books in this series with a heart-healthy theme: *Heart-healthy Everyday Meals*, *Heart-healthy Soups & Stews* and *Heart-healthy Snacks*.

acknowledgements

I would like to thank Audrey for this opportunity, as well as Le Creuset and WMF for their support and the products used in this book; my daughter Mishalle, for all the hours of baking fun and for being the real inspiration in our family; my husband, A for the unabated faith in me, you are my rock; my mother, for instilling in me the love for good food through her wonderful creations.

apple oatmeal crisp Serves 4

An apple a day really keeps the doctor away, as it contains nutrients and antioxidants that prevent damage to heart vessels. Oats help to lower total cholesterol level and regulates blood glucose levels. These two ingredients are combined here to make the perfect dessert that is healthy and tasty.

INGREDIENTS

Whole wheat flour	$1/2$ cup
Rolled oats	1 cup
Brown sugar	$1/2$ cup
Salt	a pinch
Unsalted butter	3 Tbsp, cold
Granny Smith apples	2, large, peeled and diced
Ground cinnamon	1 Tbsp
Raisins	1 Tbsp

METHOD

- Preheat oven to 180°C (350°F).

- Mix flour with oats, brown sugar and salt.

- Rub in butter with flour mixture until crumbly.

- In a separate bowl, mix apples with cinnamon and raisins.

- Divide apple mixture among four ramekins.

- Pour crumble on top of apple mixture.

- Bake for about 30 minutes or until golden brown.

- Serve warm, with a dollop of low fat plain yoghurt or crème fraîche if desired.

bread and butter pudding Serves 8

The traditional bread and butter pudding is tweaked in this healthier version. This is satisfying, yet low in fat.

INGREDIENTS

Unsalted butter	1 Tbsp
Wholemeal seeded bread	6 slices
Ground cinnamon	1 tsp
Raisins	2 Tbsp
Low fat milk	300 ml (10 fl oz / 1 1/4 cups)
Raw sugar	2 Tbsp
Vanilla extract	1 tsp
Salt	1/4 tsp
Eggs	2, large, beaten
Pistachios	2 Tbsp, shelled and chopped
Almond flakes	2 Tbsp

METHOD

- Preheat oven to 180°C (350°F).

- Spread a thin layer of butter on bread slices.

- Cut each bread slice into four triangles. Divide among eight ramekins and arrange them neatly, or place all on a greased rectangular dish. Sprinkle cinnamon and raisins in between each layer of bread.

- Prepare custard. In a heavy-bottomed pan, simmer milk with sugar, vanilla and salt over low heat.

- Add eggs and whisk gently until custard is slightly thickened.

- Pour custard over bread slices. Sprinkle pistachios and almond flakes on top.

- Bake the pudding for 20 minutes if in ramekins, or 40–45 minutes if using a rectangular dish.

- Serve immediately.

dark chocolate walnut brownies
Makes a 20-cm (8-in) cake

Use good quality dark chocolate that contain flavonoids, which are powerful antioxidants that fight diseases. This version gives the classic brownie a twist of novelty with the use of olive oil and apple purée.

INGREDIENTS

Good quality dark chocolate, at least 56% cocoa	185 g ($6^2/_3$ oz)
Extra virgin olive oil	50 ml ($1^2/_3$ fl oz)
Plain (all-purpose) flour	80 g ($2^4/_5$ oz), sifted
Salt	$^1/_8$ tsp
Cocoa powder	1 tsp
Eggs	2, beaten
Apple purée	100 g ($3^1/_2$ oz)
Raw sugar	65 g ($2^1/_3$ oz)
Low fat milk	2 Tbsp
Walnuts	75 g ($2^2/_3$ oz), lightly toasted

NOTE
To make apple purée, stew 2 apples, peeled and cored, in $^1/_2$ cup water until apples are tender. Blend or mash until smooth.

METHOD

- Preheat oven to 180°C (350°F).

- Melt chocolate with olive oil over indirect heat. Use a double boiler or a clean, dry heatproof bowl that sits snugly over a pot of simmering water.

- Meanwhile, mix flour with salt and cocoa powder. Set flour mixture aside.

- Once chocolate has melted, add eggs, apple purée, sugar and milk. Whisk until well combined.

- Fold in flour mixture.

- Add walnuts and mix well.

- Transfer batter to a 20 × 20-cm (8 × 8-in) square baking tray lined with greaseproof paper. Bake for 35 minutes.

- Cool brownies in the closed oven for 10 minutes after baking.

- Once cooled, cut into squares and serve.

caramelised banana splits Serves 2

Nuts contain omega-3-fatty acids and Vitamin E, which help prevent plaque formation in the arteries.

INGREDIENTS

Bananas	2, large, peeled
Brown sugar	1 Tbsp
Ground cinnamon	1 tsp
Extra virgin olive oil	1 tsp
Low fat vanilla ice-cream	2 scoops
Roasted walnuts	3 Tbsp, chopped

METHOD

• Cut bananas into thin rounds and place on a baking tray.

• Mix brown sugar with cinnamon and olive oil.

• Rub sugar mixture on both sides of the banana slices.

• Cook banana slices on a griddle or pan for about 8 minutes, until they are caramelised.

• Leave banana slices to cool slightly.

• Place a scoop of ice-cream in each serving glass.

• Garnish with caramelised banana slices and sprinkle with chopped walnuts.

• Serve immediately.

carrot pistachio bundts Serves 8

Carrots are a good source of beta-carotene and vitamin A, which protect against various diseases. The other main ingredient, pistachios, help to lower total blood cholesterol level.

INGREDIENTS

Dark brown sugar	$^3/_4$ cup
Eggs	2, large
Canola oil	85 ml ($2^1/_2$ fl oz / $^1/_3$ cup)
Plain (all-purpose) flour	I cup, sifted
Carrots	I cup, peeled and grated
Salt	$^1/_2$ tsp
Ground cinnamon	I tsp
Baking powder	I tsp
Pistachios	$^1/_2$ cup, lightly toasted and chopped

METHOD

- In a stand mixer, beat sugar and eggs until pale and fluffy.

- Preheat oven to 170°C (338°F).

- With the whisk still beating the mixture, add oil gradually. Continue whisking until well combined.

- In a separate bowl, combine flour, carrots, salt, cinnamon and baking powder.

- Fold flour mixture into egg batter and combine well.

- Spoon batter into greased bundt tin. Fill up the three-quarters full for each cup. Sprinkle pistachios over the batter.

- Bake for 18 minutes.

- Serve warm.

chocolate corn flakes
Makes at least 24 petit fours

These small confectionaries are called petit fours in French. Satisfying for all ages, this treat comes in the form of healthy cereals covered with fragrant dark chocolate.

INGREDIENTS

Good quality dark chocolate, at least 56% cocoa	200 g (7 oz)
Honey	2 Tbsp
Unsalted butter	1 tsp
Corn flakes	200 g (7 oz)

METHOD

- Melt chocolate over indirect heat. Use a double boiler or a clean, dry heatproof bowl that sits snugly over a pot of simmering water.

- Once chocolate has melted, add honey and butter. Stir until well combined and glossy.

- In a mixing bowl, mix corn flakes with chocolate sauce until well coated.

- Spoon chocolate corn flakes into petit four cases.

- Allow to cool before serving. The remainder can be kept refrigerated for up to 1 week.

dark chocolate almond torte
Makes a 20-cm (8-in) round cake

For such a rich and indulgent dessert, this almond torte is surprisingly low in fat. It is also suitable for vegetarians as it is gluten free.

INGREDIENTS

Good quality dark chocolate, at least 56% cocoa	180 g (6$\frac{1}{3}$ oz)
Honey	2 Tbsp
Extra virgin olive oil	100 ml (3$\frac{1}{3}$ fl oz)
Eggs	3, large, yolks and whites separated
Dark brown sugar	$\frac{1}{2}$ cup
Ground almonds	140 g (5 oz)
Baking powder	1 tsp
Cocoa powder (optional)	for dusting

METHOD

- Preheat oven to 175°C (347°F).

- Melt chocolate with honey and olive oil over indirect heat. Use a double boiler or a clean, dry heatproof bowl that sits snugly over a pot of simmering water.

- In a separate bowl, beat egg yolks with $\frac{1}{4}$ cup sugar until pale and fluffy. Add this to the chocolate and mix well.

- Combine ground almonds with baking powder, then fold into chocolate mixture.

- Using a mixer, beat egg whites with remaining $\frac{1}{4}$ cup brown sugar until stiff peaks form.

- Gently fold in egg whites into chocolate batter.

- Pour batter into a 20-cm (8-in) round pan and bake for about 35 minutes, until cracks have formed on top of the cake.

- Once cooled, generously sprinkle cocoa powder on top if desired and serve.

chocolate cherry almond clafoutis Serves 6

Clafoutis are French desserts made from cherries and fragrant batter. Cherries are rich in antioxidants and complements dark chocolate well in this scrumptious dessert.

INGREDIENTS

Good quality dark chocolate, at least 56% cocoa	100 g (3^1/$_2$ oz)
Eggs	2, large, beaten
Raw sugar	40 g (1^1/$_3$ oz)
Ground almonds	110 g (4 oz)
Self-raising flour	85 g (3 oz)
Salt	a pinch
Semi-skimmed milk	200 ml (6^3/$_4$ fl oz)
Cherries	100 g (3^1/$_2$ oz), pitted

METHOD

• Preheat oven to 180°C (350°F).

• Melt chocolate over indirect heat. Use a double boiler or a clean, dry heatproof bowl that sits snugly over a pot of simmering water.

• In a bowl, whisk eggs with sugar. Do not overbeat; stop once mixture is well combined and almost pale.

• Add ground almonds, flour, salt, milk and melted chocolate.

• Fold in cherries and mix well.

• Transfer batter into a greased tart dish or individual ramekins. Fill up to three-quarters full.

• Bake for 15 minutes if using a large tart dish, or 12 minutes if using ramekins, until the clafoutis are just set but not firm.

• Enjoy the clafoutis while they are slightly warm.

date and walnut loaf

Makes a 17.5 x 7.5-cm (7 x 3-in) loaf

Dates make healthy snacks, as they are high in fibre and other nutrients that promote overall well-being. This tasty tea-time loaf combines the pleasant sweetness of dates and the satisfying crunch of walnuts.

INGREDIENTS

Medjool dates	1 1/2 cups, pitted
Boiling water	1 cup
Plain (all-purpose) flour	1 1/2 cups
Rolled oats	4 Tbsp
Baking powder	1 tsp
Bicarbonate of soda	1/2 tsp
Dark brown sugar	4 Tbsp
Walnuts	1 cup, chopped

METHOD

- Soak dates in boiling water for 30 minutes until mushy.

- Preheat oven to 170°C (338°F).

- In a bowl, combine flour with oats, baking powder, bicarbonate of soda and sugar.

- Add dates, followed by walnuts.

- Mix well and pour batter into a greased 17.5 x 7.5-cm (7 x 3-in) loaf pan.

- Bake for 40 minutes, or until a skewer inserted into the centre of the loaf comes out clean.

date, walnut and chocolate truffles Makes 24 petit fours

Three great ingredients rich in antioxidants are combined to create these gourmet truffles.

INGREDIENTS

Dark chocolate buttons	$^1/_2$ cup
Walnuts	1 cup, lightly toasted
Medjool dates	2 cups, pitted
Honey	3 Tbsp
Cocoa powder	1 Tbsp
Cocoa powder, chocolate rice or desiccated coconut	to taste

METHOD

• Melt chocolate buttons over indirect heat. Use a double boiler or a clean, dry heatproof bowl that sits snugly over a pot of simmering water. Set aside to cool.

• In a blender, whizz walnuts, dates, honey and cocoa powder until a sticky mixture is formed.

• Mix in melted chocolate.

• Roll mixture into small balls.

• Coat balls with cocoa powder, chocolate rice or desiccated coconut.

• Serve immediately. The remainder can be kept refrigerated for up to 1 week or frozen for up to several months.

fig pecan cake Makes a 20-cm (8-in) round cake

Fig is a good source of iron, magnesium and Vitamin B, all of which build up the immune system and help to regulate heart rhythm. The nutty flavour of pecans goes well with the sweet aroma of figs in this cake.

INGREDIENTS

Eggs	2, large
Low fat plain yoghurt	250 ml (8 fl oz / 1 cup)
Extra virgin olive oil	180 ml (6 fl oz / $^3/_4$ cup)
Plain (all-purpose) flour	2 cups, sifted
Salt	1 tsp
Baking powder	1 tsp
Bicarbonate of soda	1 tsp
Dark brown sugar	$^3/_4$ cup
Figs	1 cup, chopped
Pecans	$^3/_4$ cup, chopped

METHOD

- Preheat oven to 175°C (347°F).

- In a bowl, whisk eggs with yoghurt and olive oil until almost fluffy.

- In a separate bowl, combine flour with salt, baking powder, bicarbonate of soda and brown sugar.

- Add figs and pecan, and coat them well with flour mixture.

- Slowly drizzle in egg mixture and mix well.

- Pour batter into a greased 20-cm (8-in) round pan and bake for 35–40 minutes, or until a skewer inserted into the centre of the cake comes out clean.

mixed fruit and nut flapjacks
Makes about 12 flapjacks

These flapjacks, or oat bars, are packed with nutrients and vitamins from fruit, nuts and olive oil.
Enjoy goodness on the go with these healthy and yummy energy boosters.

INGREDIENTS

Rolled oats	240 g (8 1/2 oz)
Raisins	50 g (1 2/3 oz)
Dried cranberries	30 g (1 oz)
Almonds	50 g (1 2/3 oz)
Pistachios	50 g (1 2/3 oz), shelled
Unsalted butter	30 g (1 oz)
Honey	50 ml (1 2/3 fl oz)
Extra virgin olive oil	100 ml (3 1/3 fl oz)
Dark brown sugar	60 g (2 oz)
Salt	1/8 tsp
Cardamom pods	3
Ground cinnamon	1 tsp
Sesame seeds	2 Tbsp
Almond flakes	4 Tbsp

METHOD

- Preheat oven to 180°C (350°F).

- Combine oats, dried fruits and nuts in a mixing bowl.

- Prepare syrup. In a saucepan, melt butter with honey, olive oil, brown sugar, salt, cardamom pods and cinnamon.

- Pour syrup onto dry ingredients and mix until everything is well coated with syrup and sticky.

- Press mixture into a greased 20 x 20-cm (8 x 8-in) square baking tray.

- Sprinkle sesame seeds and almond flakes on top.

- Bake for 25 minutes or until golden brown.

- Once cooled, cut into squares and serve. The remainder can be kept refrigerated for up to a month.

Officially the City and County of San Francisco

SAN FRANCISCO

fruit salad Serves 4

A perennial favourite, the fruit salad allows guilt-free indulgence for those with a sweet tooth. Rich in vitamin C and trace minerals, fruits help in wound-healing and protect heart vessels from further plaque formation.

INGREDIENTS

Pomegranate arils (seeds)	from 1 pomegranate
Apples	2, cored and cubed
Strawberries	5, hulled and sliced
Blueberries	$1/2$ cup
Kiwi	$1/2$ cup, peeled and cubed
Pineapple slices	$1/2$ cup, cut into bite-size pieces
Tangerines	4, small, peeled and cut into bite-size pieces
Lemon	1, for juice and zest
Mint leaves	a few, coarsely chopped
Honey	1 Tbsp

METHOD

• In a large salad bowl, mix all the fruits, except pomegranate arils, together with lemon zest and mint leaves.

• Mix honey with lemon juice and drizzle over fruits.

• Scatter pomegranate arils over and mix well.

• Divide among serving glasses and serve immediately.

honey lemon popsicles Makes 4 popsicles

Low in fat and chock-full of antioxidants, these popsicles are easy to make and are better than store-bought ones anytime.

INGREDIENTS

Lemons	4, large, for juice, peel and zest
Water	500 ml (16 fl oz / 2 cups)
Honey	125 ml (4 fl oz / 1/2 cup)

METHOD

• Juice lemons for 250 ml (8 fl oz / 1 cup) of juice. Reserve lemon zest and peel.

• Simmer lemon juice with water, lemon zest and honey until boiling point.

• Pour mixture into popsicle moulds and throw in some lemon peel.

• Freeze for at least 6 hours or overnight until firm.

honey roasted plums Serves 4–6

Juicy and sweet, this cheery-looking treat brightens up any day and can be prepared in no time at all.

INGREDIENTS

Honey	3 Tbsp
Extra virgin olive oil	1 Tbsp
Lemon juice	from ½ lemon
Cinnamon stick	1
Ground cinnamon	1 tsp
Star anise	2
Kosher salt	a pinch
Plums	4, halved and pitted

METHOD

- Preheat oven to 180°C (350°F).

- Prepare syrup. Mix honey with olive oil, lemon juice, cinnamon stick, ground cinnamon and star anise.

- Pour syrup into a shallow baking tray and sprinkle salt over.

- Place plums, with cut side down, on syrup.

- Bake for 30 minutes.

- Enjoy roasted plums on its own or with low fat vanilla ice-cream if desired.

lemon madeleines Makes about 12 madeleines

This classic French delicacy gets a healthy makeover with the use of lemon and olive oil.

INGREDIENTS

Extra virgin olive oil	4 Tbsp + 1 tsp for greasing pan
Plain (all-purpose) flour	1 tsp
Eggs	3, large
Castor sugar	1/2 cup
Lemon zest	from 1 lemon
Lemon juice	2 Tbsp
Self-raising flour	1/2 cup, sifted
Baking powder	1 tsp

METHOD

- Preheat oven to 180°C (350°F).

- Grease madeleine pan with oil, then dust pan with plain flour.

- In a stand mixer, beat eggs with sugar until it triples in volume and is fluffy.

- Combine lemon zest, lemon juice and olive oil, then drizzle onto egg batter with the whisk still beating the mixture.

- Mix self-raising flour with baking powder, then fold gently into batter using a spatula. Be careful not to knock air out of the batter; this is to ensure that the volume is retained.

- Allow batter to sit for 30 minutes.

- Spoon batter into a greased madeleine pan until each mould is three-quarters full.

- Bake for 10–12 minutes, until madeleines are puffed and golden with crispy edges.

mango mascarpone verrine Serves 4

Contrary to popular belief that they are too sugary and therefore bad for the heart, mangoes
actually contain essential antioxidants and minerals that are good for nerve and muscle functions.
This recipe uses low fat dairy products with mango to make a nice fruity treat.

INGREDIENTS

Low fat mascarpone cheese	250 ml (8 fl oz / 1 cup)
Honey	3 Tbsp
Cardamom seeds	from a few pods
Mangoes	2, large, peeled and cubed
Low fat plain Greek yoghurt	250 ml (8 fl oz / 1 cup)

METHOD

- Beat mascarpone cheese with honey and cardamom seeds until almost fluffy.

- In a blender, purée half of the mango cubes until smooth.

- Layer the bottom of each serving glass with mango purée, followed by mascarpone cheese, until a third full.

- Spoon another layer of mango purée, followed by yoghurt.

- Keep layering until glass is full.

- Garnish with remaining mango cubes and serve chilled.

very berry meringue nest
Makes about 12 nests

This meringue dessert is called a pavlova, a creation in honour of the Russian ballerina, Anna Pavlova. Egg white is a main ingredient here. It contains protein (albumin), and is the healthiest part of the egg. The crisp nest is complemented by bright juicy fruits rich in antioxidants and vitamins, a delicious treat that never fails to satisfy.

INGREDIENTS

Egg whites	from 4 large eggs
Cream of tartar	$^1/_2$ tsp
Vanilla extract	1 tsp
Golden castor sugar	4 Tbsp
Mixed berries (blueberries, strawberries and raspberries)	as desired

METHOD

- Preheat oven to 130°C (266°F).

- Prepare meringue. In a stand mixer, whip egg whites and cream of tartar.

- Once fluffy, add vanilla extract and sugar. Beat until stiff peaks form.

- Gently fold meringue into a pastry bag fitted with a star-shaped nozzle, and pipe a nest of about 6 cm (2.5 in) in diameter on a greased baking tray.

- Bake meringue nests for about 1 hour, or until they are firm and dry.

- Once baked, leave the nests to rest in the oven with the door closed for another hour.

- Fill the nest with mixed berries and serve. The remainder can be stored in an airtight container for up to 3 days.

dark chocolate orange mousse Serves 6–8

Chocolate and orange both provide antioxidants and minerals essential for a healthy heart. This mousse is great as an after-dinner dessert, and is perfect for entertaining.

INGREDIENTS

Good quality dark chocolate, at least 56% cocoa	200 g (7 oz)
Low fat non-dairy whipping cream	85 ml (2$^1/_2$ fl oz / $^1/_3$ cup)
Orange juice and zest	from 2 oranges
Orange extract	1 tsp
Orange peel (optional)	for garnishing

METHOD

- Melt chocolate over indirect heat. Use a double boiler or a clean, dry heatproof bowl that sits snugly over a pot of simmering water.

- Whip cream until fluffy.

- Add melted chocolate, orange juice, zest and extract.

- Transfer into serving cups.

- Refrigerate for 2–4 hours to let the mousse set.

- Serve chilled, with orange peel if desired.

vanilla panna cotta with strawberry compote Serves 4-6

Tasty and easy to make, this Italian cream dessert can be enjoyed during gatherings. This recipe promises a guilt-free indulgence with low fat dairy products and fruity compote, which is made from fresh fruits stewed in syrup.

INGREDIENTS

Gelatin powder	1 Tbsp
Water	4 Tbsp
Semi-skimmed milk	250 ml (8 fl oz / 1 cup)
Raw sugar	50 g (1²/₃ oz)
Vanilla pod	1, seeds scrapped and pod reserved
Low fat plain Greek yoghurt	375 ml (12 fl oz / 1¹/₂ cups)
Strawberries	400 g (14 oz), hulled and sliced
Sugar	1 Tbsp
Balsamic vinegar	a few drops

METHOD

• Sprinkle gelatin into water, then whisk mixture over indirect heat until gelatin has fully dissolved. Use a double boiler or a clean, dry heatproof bowl that sits snugly over a pot of simmering water.

• In a heavy-bottomed pan, simmer milk with raw sugar, vanilla seeds and pod.

• Once sugar has dissolved and milk is simmering, remove from heat. Discard vanilla pod, then add gelatin solution.

• Whisk vigorously and add yoghurt. Whisk until well combined.

• Spoon panna cotta mixture into jelly moulds and refrigerate for at least 6 hours, or until firm.

• Prepare strawberry compote. Stew strawberries with sugar and balsamic vinegar over low heat, with the pan covered. After about 5 minutes, when the mixture turns syrupy, remove from heat.

• Remove panna cotta from moulds and serve with strawberry compote.

peach sorbet Serves 8

Homemade sorbet is surprisingly easy to make. It is not only healthy but also contains no preservatives. This recipe can be used with any fruit that is in season. Replace peaches with other fruits of your choice if desired.

INGREDIENTS

Peaches	4 cups, peeled and diced
Honey	2 Tbsp
Lemon juice	from 1 lemon
Raw sugar	$1/2$ cup
Salt	$1/4$ tsp

METHOD

- In a blender, purée peaches with honey, lemon and sugar.

- Strain purée and add salt to the mixture.

- Transfer purée to a container and freeze for 3 hours.

- Churn mixture in an ice-cream maker, then serve immediately. If a firmer texture is preferred, freeze again after churning, until desired firmness is achieved before serving.

- Alternatively, if an ice-cream maker is not available, freeze mixture for 3 hours, then churn in a stand mixer with a paddle attachment for 5 minutes, followed by a whisk attachment for 10 minutes until fluffy. Freeze again for 3 hours, then repeat churning cycle. Freeze for 3 hours, then serve immediately.

vanilla spice poached pear with dark chocolate sauce Serves 4

Generous consumption of pear prevents high blood pressure, stroke and heart diseases.
Complement this fragrant poached pear with rich chocolate sauce for a healthy indulgence.

INGREDIENTS

Ripe packham pears	4, peeled
Cinnamon stick	1
Cloves	3
Star anise	2
Lemon zest	from 1 lemon
Honey	2 Tbsp
Vanilla pod	1
Good quality dark chocolate, at least 56% cocoa	100 g (3 1/2 oz)

METHOD

- In a heavy-bottomed pan, arrange pears with all the spices, lemon zest and honey.

- Fill the pan with water until pears are submerged.

- Scrape vanilla seeds into the pan, adding in the pod as well.

- Simmer for about 20 minutes, until pears are soft.

- Meanwhile, melt chocolate over indirect heat. Use a double boiler or a clean, dry heatproof bowl that sits snugly over a pot of simmering water.

- Place poached pears on serving plates and drizzle with hot melted chocolate. Serve immediately.

pomegranate jello Serves 4

Pomegranates contain high levels of flavonoids and antioxidants, which protect against heart diseases. This jello is easy to make and brings out the flavour of pomegranate in every spoonful.

INGREDIENTS

Freshly squeezed pomegranate juice	1 litre (32 fl oz / 4 cups)
Gelatin powder	10 g ($^1/_3$ oz)
Honey	2 Tbsp
Pomegranate arils (seeds)	$^3/_4$ cup

METHOD

• Pour a quarter of the pomegranate juice into a cup and sprinkle gelatin powder on top. Let gelatin mixture sit for 5 minutes.

• In a pan, heat remaining pomegranate juice with honey until it simmers.

• Add gelatin mixture and stir until gelatin has fully dissolved.

• At this stage, pour in pomegranate arils. Alternatively, reserve them for garnishing if desired.

• Pour liquid into tall serving glasses or moulds and refrigerate for 8 hours, until jello has set.

• Serve chilled.

raisin scones Makes 6 scones

A healthier version of this British classic is made using wholemeal flour and oats, which are rich in fibre and contain high amounts of omega-3 fatty acids. Apart from these additional nutrients, these ingredients give a new delicious flavour to the scones.

INGREDIENTS

Wholemeal flour	$1/2$ cup
Cake flour	$1/2$ cup
Baking powder	2 tsp
Rolled oats	$1/2$ cup, finely ground
Salt	a pinch
Raw sugar	3 Tbsp + 1 tsp for topping
Unsalted butter	4 Tbsp, cold
Raisins	4 Tbsp
Egg	1
Low fat milk	85 ml ($2^1/2$ fl oz / $1/3$ cup) + 1 Tbsp for brushing dough
Raw sugar	1 tsp
Crème fraîche	as desired
Fresh fruits	as desired

METHOD

- Preheat oven to 190°C (375°F).

- In a large bowl, mix both flours, baking powder, oats, salt and sugar.

- Rub in cold butter until mixture is crumbly.

- Fold in raisins.

- Beat egg with milk, and combine with mixture above.

- Shape dough by hand such that it is about 4 cm (1.5 in) thick.

- Using a round cutter, cut dough into 5-cm (2-in) circles and place on a greased baking tray.

- Brush the top with milk and sprinkle sugar over as topping.

- Bake for about 15 minutes, until scones have risen and are golden yellow.

- Serve scones with crème fraîche and fresh fruits.

raspberry friands
Makes about 12 small cakes

These small moist cakes are a French classic, made healthier by using egg whites. Rich in minerals from almonds and raspberries, this delicious treat is perfect for entertaining or as a festive gift.

INGREDIENTS

Egg whites	from 5 large eggs
Icing (confectioner's) sugar	50 g (1 2/3 oz) + 1 Tbsp for dusting
Plain (all-purpose) flour	55 g (2 oz), sifted
Ground almonds	120 g (4 1/3 oz)
Lemon extract	1 tsp
Butter	85 g (3 oz), melted
Raspberries	150 g (5 1/3 oz)

METHOD

• Preheat oven to 180°C (350°F).

• Whisk egg whites with icing sugar until soft peaks form.

• Add flour, ground almonds, lemon extract and melted butter.

• Combine well and fold in raspberries.

• Spoon batter into greased friand mould or muffin pans.

• Bake for 20–25 minutes until golden.

• Once cool, dust with icing sugar just before serving.

rice krispies Makes 24 bars

The addition of apples boosts flavour. Use fat-free marshmallows for a healthier version.

INGREDIENTS

Green apple	1, large, peeled and chopped
Canola oil	1 Tbsp
Fat-free marshmallows	¹/₂ cup
Honey	3 Tbsp
Rice krispies	2 cups

METHOD

• Stew chopped apple with a dash of water until soft, then purée in a blender.

• In a saucepan, heat oil and melt marshmallows with honey.

• Add apple purée and rice krispies. Mix well.

• Transfer mixture into a baking tray lined with greaseproof paper. Press to distribute evenly. Set aside to cool.

• Once cooled, cut into squares and serve. These healthy bars can keep well in an airtight container for up to 2 weeks.

saffron-infused semolina pudding Serves 8

This is a favourite Middle-eastern and Continental dessert. Semolina is high in proteins that are necessary for good health. The mixed nuts not only provide crunch and flavour, but are also rich in omega-3 fatty acids.

INGREDIENTS

Saffron	10 strands
Warm low fat milk	500 ml (16 fl oz / 2 cups)
Canola oil	1 Tbsp
Cinnamon stick	1
Cloves	2
Star anise	2
Mixed nuts (almonds, pistachios, cashews)	1/4 cup
Water	250 ml (8 fl oz / 1 cup)
Fine semolina	1 cup
Raw sugar	4 Tbsp
Raisins	4 Tbsp
Salt	1/4 tsp

METHOD

- Soak saffron strands in warm milk for at least 30 minutes, until the milk becomes golden yellow in colour.

- In a heavy-bottomed pan, heat oil and add cinnamon, cloves, star anise and mixed nuts.

- Once spices are fragrant, add milk and water, and let it simmer.

- Add semolina, sugar, raisins and salt.

- Simmer on low heat until it thickens.

- Serve warm or chilled in glasses.

strawberries in dark chocolate fondue Serves 20

This fuss-free dessert is a definite crowd-pleaser with molten dark chocolate.

INGREDIENTS

Single (light) cream	185 ml (6¼ fl oz)
Good quality dark chocolate, at least 56% cocoa	200 g (7 oz)
Strawberries	400 g (14 oz), hulled

FLAVOURING

Vanilla extract	1 tsp
or	
Orange zest	from 1 orange

METHOD

- In a saucepan, heat cream until it simmers.

- Pour heated cream over chocolate in a bowl.

- Mix until chocolate has melted and a smooth ganache is formed.

- Stir in flavouring of choice.

- Transfer ganache into a fondue pot so it remains liquid. Alternatively, fill a pan or griddle with hot water to create a hot water bath. Transfer ganache into a ceramic or metal bowl, and place it on the hot water bath to keep the ganache fluid.

- Enjoy with a platter of strawberries.

strawberry granola parfait Serves 2

These pretty-looking parfaits are deliciously healthy with the goodness of strawberries and oats.

INGREDIENTS

Low fat plain Greek yoghurt	250 ml (8 fl oz / 1 cup)
Honey	3 Tbsp
Store-bought fruity granola	1 cup
Strawberries	1 cup, hulled and sliced

N O T E

If you wish to make your own granola, refer to the mini cookbook *Heart-healthy Everyday Meals*, page 36.

METHOD

- Fill a third of each serving glass with yoghurt.

- Spoon 1 Tbsp honey on top, followed by granola.

- Arrange few slices of strawberries on top, followed by yoghurt.

- Repeat layers until ingredients are used up.

- Garnish with strawberries.

- Serve chilled.

strawberry-peach popsicles Makes 4 popsicles

Strawberries and peaches go well together to give a unique flavour. These refreshing popsicles contain all the good things from their fruity ingredients—antioxidants, vitamins and great taste.

INGREDIENTS

Strawberries	200 g (7 oz), hulled and chopped
White peaches	4, large, peeled and chopped
Raw sugar	3 Tbsp
Spring water	4 Tbsp
Ice-cream sticks	4

METHOD

• Purée all ingredients in a blender until smooth.

• Pour into popsicle moulds and freeze for about 6 hours or until firm. Halfway through the freezing process, after about 3 hours, insert ice-cream sticks into half-frozen popsicles.

• Remove from moulds and indulge.

strawberry smoothies Serves 2

These yummy smoothies are perfect for any time of the day, and is chock-full of antioxidants.

INGREDIENTS

Strawberries	1 cup, hulled
Low fat plain Greek yoghurt	125 ml (4 fl oz / $^1/_2$ cup)
Low fat milk	125 ml (4 fl oz / $^1/_2$ cup)
Honey	1 Tbsp
Wheat germ	1 Tbsp
Ice cubes	a few

METHOD

• Whizz all the ingredients in a blender until smooth.

• Serve chilled in glasses.

strawberry tart

Makes a 28 x 18 x 5-cm (11 x 7 x 2-in) tart

Enjoy a richly-flavoured tart with fresh strawberries as the key player and a delicious biscuit-like base, a healthy crust made from whole wheat flour.

INGREDIENTS

CRUST

Whole wheat flour	200 g (7 oz)
Extra virgin olive oil	30 ml (1 fl oz)
Egg yolk	1
Raw sugar	2 Tbsp
Salt	1/4 tsp
Cold water	2–3 Tbsp

FILLING

Low fat non-dairy whipping cream	250 ml (8 fl oz / 1 cup)
Strawberries	300 g (10 1/2 oz), hulled and sliced
Honey	3 Tbsp

METHOD

- Prepare dough for the crust. In a large mixing bowl, combine flour with olive oil, egg yolk, sugar and salt. Combine well and add water to form a smooth dough.

- Chill dough for 30 minutes to 1 hour.

- Preheat oven to 190°C (375°F).

- Roll dough to fit a 28 x 18 x 5-cm (11 x 7 x 2-in) rectangular pan, or a 20-cm (8-in) round pan.

- Blind bake the crust. Prick dough all over with a fork. Place greaseproof paper on top of the dough and evenly distribute baking weights over the base. Dried beans or uncooked grains can be baking weights. Baking weights prevent the base from being uneven or weakened.

- Bake for 25 minutes or until golden brown. Set aside to cool.

- Meanwhile, whip cream until fluffy.

- Pipe cream onto cooled crust and arrange strawberry slices neatly on top.

- Drizzle with honey for extra sheen and serve.

vanilla fro-yo Serves 4

Forget the store-bought version. This frozen yoghurt is so easy to make, and it's delicious too.

INGREDIENTS

Honey	4 Tbsp
Vanilla seeds	scraped from 1 vanilla pod
Low fat plain Greek yoghurt	500 ml (16 fl oz / 2 cups)
Chopped nuts	as desired

METHOD

• Heat honey with vanilla seeds and pod until simmering.

• Cool honey mixture, then discard the vanilla pod and add in cold yoghurt.

• Mix well and transfer to a container. Freeze for about 3 hours.

• Churn mixture in an ice-cream maker.

• Serve as soft scoop frozen yoghurt ice-cream, or freeze for another few hours until it reaches desired firmness.

• Garnish with chopped nuts and enjoy.

watermelon granita Serves 4

Surprise and impress with these gorgeous crystals of iced watermelon, a dessert perfect for entertaining guests.

INGREDIENTS

Chopped watermelons	3 cups
Honey	1 Tbsp
Lemon juice	from $1/2$ lemon
Spring water	125 ml (8 fl oz / $1/2$ cup)

METHOD

- In a blender, whizz all ingredients until smooth.

- Pour liquid onto a shallow tray and freeze for 2 hours.

- Using a fork, fluff the semi-frozen mixture until it resembles crystal beads in texture.

- Freeze again for another 4–6 hours.

- Fluff with a fork again and serve.

blood orange agar agar Serves 4

Compared to regular oranges, the juice and flesh of blood oranges are crimson and darker, and it also contains a higher amount of vitamin C. Agar agar literally contains no fat. Paired with blood oranges, this soothing dessert packs loads of vitamin C and antioxidants, which have healing properties and help to counter diseases.

INGREDIENTS

Water	4 Tbsp
Raw sugar	4 Tbsp
Agar agar powder	2 tsp
Blood orange juice	from 2 blood oranges
Orange juice	from 4 Valencia oranges

METHOD

- Boil water with raw sugar and agar agar powder, until everything has fully dissolved.

- Add both orange juices, then simmer for another 5 minutes on medium-low heat.

- Pour liquid into jelly moulds and refrigerate until firm.

- Serve chilled.

weights and measures

Quantities for this book are given in Metric, Imperial and American (spoon and cup) measures. Standard spoon and cup measurements used are: 1 tsp = 5 ml, 1 Tbsp = 15 ml, 1 cup = 250 ml. All measures are level unless otherwise stated.

Liquid And Volume Measures

Metric	Imperial	American
5 ml	1/6 fl oz	1 teaspoon
10 ml	1/3 fl oz	1 dessertspoon
15 ml	1/2 fl oz	1 tablespoon
60 ml	2 fl oz	1/4 cup (4 tablespoons)
85 ml	2 1/2 fl oz	1/3 cup
90 ml	3 fl oz	3/8 cup (6 tablespoons)
125 ml	4 fl oz	1/2 cup
180 ml	6 fl oz	3/4 cup
250 ml	8 fl oz	1 cup
300 ml	10 fl oz (1/2 pint)	1 1/4 cups
375 ml	12 fl oz	1 1/2 cups
435 ml	14 fl oz	1 3/4 cups
500 ml	16 fl oz	2 cups
625 ml	20 fl oz (1 pint)	2 1/2 cups
750 ml	24 fl oz (1 1/5 pints)	3 cups
1 litre	32 fl oz (1 3/5 pints)	4 cups
1.25 litres	40 fl oz (2 pints)	5 cups
1.5 litres	48 fl oz (2 2/5 pints)	6 cups
2.5 litres	80 fl oz (4 pints)	10 cups

Dry Measures

Metric	Imperial
30 grams	1 ounce
45 grams	1 1/2 ounces
55 grams	2 ounces
70 grams	2 1/2 ounces
85 grams	3 ounces
100 grams	3 1/2 ounces
110 grams	4 ounces
125 grams	4 1/2 ounces
140 grams	5 ounces
280 grams	10 ounces
450 grams	16 ounces (1 pound)
500 grams	1 pound, 1 1/2 ounces
700 grams	1 1/2 pounds
800 grams	1 3/4 pounds
1 kilogram	2 pounds, 3 ounces
1.5 kilograms	3 pounds, 4 1/2 ounces
2 kilograms	4 pounds, 6 ounces

Oven Temperature

	°C	°F	Gas Regulo
Very slow	120	250	1
Slow	150	300	2
Moderately slow	160	325	3
Moderate	180	350	4
Moderately hot	190/200	375/400	5/6
Hot	210/220	410/425	6/7
Very hot	230	450	8
Super hot	250/290	475/550	9/10

Length

Metric	Imperial
0.5 cm	1/4 inch
1 cm	1/2 inch
1.5 cm	3/4 inch
2.5 cm	1 inch

Abbreviation

tsp	teaspoon
Tbsp	tablespoon
g	gram
kg	kilogram
ml	millilitre